T0198721

Written by: _____

Dedicated to: _____

Journaling dates: _____

Therapeutic Journaling

Making Sense of My Life

Priscilla Sobremonte

authorHOUSE®

AuthorHouse™
1663 Liberty Drive
Bloomington, IN 47403
www.authorhouse.com
Phone: 1 (800) 839-8640

Published by AuthorHouse 03/22/2018

ISBN: 978-1-5462-3431-9 (sc)
ISBN: 978-1-5462-3430-2 (e)

Introduction

The purpose of therapeutic journaling is for the user (you) to look (explore) objectively at your life experiences, which have impacted the creation and growth of your emotional, mental, physical, and spiritual uniqueness. The questions help guide you in a fact finding direction to aid you in a systematic process to look at where you have been.

Once you can look at your life objectively, then it is hoped you can normalize some of the subjectivity that oftentimes keeps us stuck in the past. Long ago a wise person advised me that, knowledge is power, therefore knowledge of you is a powerful way to release the wounds, scares, trials, lost hopes and dreams and hopefully gain insight and peace from your journey this far.

Ancient wisdom holds that to be self-actualized is to know oneself and to be oneself; which includes being present with yourself to embrace all your moments. You are a sum total of your strengths, weakness, wounds, trials, successes, failures, thoughts, feelings (both negative and positive), gifts and talents which make you unique.

We, who have struggled, only need to reflect on history. To be human is to struggle. I believe as we (humans) travel through life, we instinctively seek to know ourselves and to avoid pain and suffering. Ironically to get to know and/or accepting ourselves is the biggest life challenge we humans have to endure, which requires us to experience our suffering and learn from it.

As we live at some point we ask ourselves. Who am I? What did I do to deserve this? Why me? Why was I born? Often we look for the answers everywhere but in our divine nature. When we suffer we struggle, blame, question, seek, medicate, project, to make sense of the suffering. The truth is to suffer is to be human. When we do not know or understand ourselves: when we deny ourselves, both the good and the bad; then we lose what we were born to understand.

The point is we (humans) are both positive and negative (yin and yang) creatures. The goal of this journal is to help, you to look at your good, your bad, your ugly, and then to look at yourself objectively. I hope writing your own therapeutic journal helps you gain enlightenment into you. This is for you the user to discover the who, you really are: to become free to connect with all your thoughts, feelings, experiences, expectations of your uniqueness and then to process your wholeness and come to accept you and your experiences.

Some of the questions about yourself, early childhood history, and your families you may not be able to answer. You can ask other people who knew your family. You can go to a local library and request the library to order microfilm, newspapers, of the places you lived and grew up.

If I could fly away

So many people struggle with what should have been!
What "they" did to me and how they got me stuck in a vicious
life cycle of negativity. In my opinion healing comes from looking
at the facts of the life you have lived this far. Our lives have
valuable lessons, to teach us if we are present to the lessons...

I challenge you to take a moment of your life to ask yourself
to consider these statements "I have lived this far, what do
I need to know about myself to begin my research of me?"
"What were my expectations (my fantasy) of how my life
should have been?" "What do I need to grieve for?

Second task is to begin to live the life I have, not my fantasy.
Living with a natural kind of acceptance, just as we accept that
the ocean flows and self-cleans, so does our lives, with the good
and the bad, if we let it. Good luck on your journey back to you.

I am only looking back to find me and bring me home to me,
I could never stay there as it does not flow or grow.

With Peace and Blessings
Priscilla.

Tools that may help you while you journal

Selecting a Therapist

As you proceed on your journey back to yourself, I recommend finding a therapist that you feel comfortable, supported and feel you can trust. Therapists are licensed by a licensing agency, the licensing agency checks and ensures that the therapist has maintained a standard of practice that is safe for the public. You may also go online and find out if a therapist is in good standing or not. The reason I recommend a therapist is that he/she can help guide and support you through your healing journey. In this process, keep in mind that you are the consumer; you have a right and responsibility to obtain a provider who is professional and ethical and can best assist with this process.

I have included just a few tips to be aware if you choose to obtain a therapist. What is a healthy or unhealthy therapeutic relationship is briefly explored? Many behaviors of a potentially abusive therapist may be appropriate in a healthy therapeutic relationship. You would be advised to discuss any behaviors that you feel or think are inappropriate with the therapist before terminating therapy. For example, a therapist may appropriately, from time to time, use her/his personal experiences to illustrate a therapeutic point. A therapist may also be willing to cut fees as a way of accommodating your limited budget. A therapist may even from time to time accept a small gift from you, so long as the purpose and meaning of the gift are explored and understood. The frequency and intensity of these behaviors may mark the difference between safe and unsafe therapeutic boundaries.

The following boundary violations are danger signs that something may be seriously amiss in therapy. When these or other behaviors make you feel uncomfortable occur, do not hesitate to question what is taking place, express your discomfort, and feel free to seek another's opinion. You can ask the therapist to stop his/her behavior. You can tell a family member or friend what has happened that alarmed you. You can keep careful notes on what is happening, along with cancelled checks, insurance payment notifications, gifts she/he has given you. Most therapists are ethical and professional, just like in every profession; it is wise to be an informed consumer. If you experience behaviors that you feel are causing you harm and you have talked it over with the therapist and the incidents continue, terminate and file a complaint with the professional's licensing agency.

Some specific inappropriate behaviors could be; you are asked to listen to the therapist's sexual relationships, he/she makes sexual or suggestive jokes, ask you about your sex life that is unrelated to the issue you have come to see him/her for. The therapist wants to meet you outside of the office or professional setting. Tells you not to talk to anyone else about your therapy, it is secret, therapy is confidential between you and the therapist unless you give consent for another to have information regarding therapy, unless you are court ordered or mandated by an agency. Therapists are mandated reporters, they must report child abuse, adult/elder abuse, threats made by you to do harm to another person. These mandated situations should be told to you by the therapist at the onset of therapy. Other situations are he/she talks to you about other patients, borrow money, threaten you, promise to be your caretaker, offer alcohol and/or drugs.

Tools that may help you while you journal

CONTROL YOUR EMOTIONS AND MIND BY BREATHING:
(Please consult your health care provider before starting any new activity)

Regulating your breathing is a conscious technique that is taught for stress reduction and achieving relaxation and calmness. There are many techniques to practice conscious breathing I only included the one that has helped me in the past. Please explore and test out other breathing exercises which may suit you better.

Location is everything you have heard that before!
One of the first things to do is create an environment that you will be able to relax and not be disturbed. You can do this by finding a place that is peaceful for you and make yourself comfortable. Many people I know have set up certain places in their home that they dedicate to this practice, others pick a spot in their yard, and then others go to the beach, mountains or a park. The point is being creative, experiment and find out what works best for you. This is an all about you process.

Breath begins life.
To begin the actual breathing exercises, try to relax and settle into the place you have selected. Once you feel at ease slowly begin breathing. Start becoming aware of the way you naturally breathe in and out, discover your own unique rhythm. Take plenty of time just being one with yourself, by focusing on your breath. Once you have made a conscious effort to tune into your natural breath, you can begin slowing your breath down.

After you feel like you are consciously with your breathing rhythm just take a mental inventory of your body, is there any tension? If so give the tension some attention, feel the area of your body for a few minutes, try to connect the tension with your natural breathing rhythm, is it out of rhythm? Now direct your attention to breathing through your nose and out through your mouth with you lips slightly parted, try for the count of four to four (in four and out four counts).

So now you are relaxing and thinking about the air passing through you nose, through your chest, ending up in your diaphragm, (visualize, water fall the air cascading into the pool-your diaphragm). As you breathe in through your nose concentrate on the how the air/breath moves into your respiratory tract. Counting is often helpful; some people just focus on breathing in and out and try just to think of the breath. Others find it helpful to count; a good starting count is four counts in and four counts out.

The process breath slowly in through your nose focus on the air traveling through your body, when it reaches the diaphragm (just above your stomach) you will know it has reached your diaphragm by being mindful of your abdomen extending. Hold the breath in your abdomen, (if you are counting you can hold for the count of four if you can, do not strain yourself). The time you spend with yourself is the best times of life. Just take a few minutes of your day to practice your breathing.

This technique can help calm "Anger"

I. Slow down, take a time out, and begin to deep breath. The deep breathing can regulate and harmonize the Solar Plexus (lower emotion) located below rib cage top of stomach. Effects are to produce CALMNESS, PEACE AND SERENITY.

Process Breath in slowly through you nose fill your stomach with as much air as you can hold in, your stomach (diaphragm), for as long as you can without it being difficult.

Process Breath out slowly thinking about it moving from your stomach (diaphragm) through your chest, into your throat and out your mouth.

Try to do 12 cycles

II. To hasten the Healing Calming process. *Think positive*= when you think, feel and act positive you can being changing you programming, in time and with commitment it can become a habit. *Daily Affirmations*= for a few minutes at least for several months state a positive personal growth goal. *Visualize*= being healthy, getting healthy completely, feeling one with yourself, being happy, self-confident, kind and at peace with yourself and others.

III. Practice Meditation by sitting alone thinking of nothing just your breath, or of a pleasant place that brings you comfort, or has brought you comfort. Many people find thinking of the ocean calming.

Anger, Stress Management Tool
P. Sobremonte, L.C.S.W.
Psychiatric Social Worker

My full name is:

_____

_____

_____

_____

_____

How I feel about my name:

_____

_____

_____

_____

_____

_____

_____

_____

_____

_____

What my name means (I looked at a name book) and this is
what the name I was given means as stated by this book:

_____

_____

_____

_____

_____

_____

_____

_____

How I got the name I was given, as I was
told, it was because of this or that:

_____

_____

_____

_____

_____

_____

_____

_____

_____

_____

_____

_____

_____

_____

The name I would have liked to have been given:

_____

_____

_____

_____

_____

_____

_____

_____

_____

_____

_____

_____

_____

I wanted this name because:

_____

_____

_____

_____

_____

_____

_____

My nickname is, I was given this nickname because:

_____

_____

_____

_____

_____

_____

_____

_____

The name I secretly call myself is because:

_____

_____

_____

_____

_____

_____

_____

_____

_____

The time of day or night I was born:

_____
_____
_____
_____
_____
_____
_____
_____
_____
_____
_____
_____
_____
_____
_____
_____

The weather at the time I was born was, according
to my research. You know I really (like or
dislike) this type of weather because:

_____
_____
_____
_____
_____
_____
_____
_____
_____
_____
_____
_____
_____
_____
_____

_____

_____

_____

_____

_____

_____

_____

_____

_____

_____

_____

_____

_____

My birthday is and this is what was happening in the world
when I was born, as I have discovered from my research:

_____

_____

_____

_____

_____

_____

_____

_____

_____

_____

_____

_____

_____

_____

_____

_____

_____

_____

_____

_____

_____

_____

_____

_____

_____

_____

_____

_____

_____

_____

_____

_____

My birthplace was. This is what I know about
my birthplace, or this is what I have found out
since I have been writing this journal:

_____

_____

_____

_____

_____

_____

_____

_____

_____

_____

_____

_____

_____

_____

_____

_____

_____

_____

_____

_____

_____

_____

_____

_____

_____

_____

_____

_____

_____

My astrological sign is, my Chinese horoscope, my
Numerology Number is. What I was told about this
these things. What they mean to me or not and why:

_____

_____

_____

_____

_____

_____

_____

_____

_____

_____

_____

_____

_____

_____

_____

_____

_____

_____

_____

_____

_____

_____

_____

_____

_____

_____

_____

_____

My earliest memories of my life are:

_____

_____

_____

_____

_____

_____

_____

_____

_____

_____

_____

_____

_____

_____

_____

_____

_____

_____

_____

_____

_____

_____

_____

_____

_____

_____

_____

_____

_____

_____

When I was a baby, this is what I was told I was about myself:

_____

_____

_____

_____

_____

_____

_____

_____

_____

_____

_____

_____

_____

_____

_____

_____

_____

_____

_____

_____

_____

_____

_____

_____

_____

_____

_____

_____

_____

_____

_____

_____

What I think people thought about me as a child:

_____

_____

_____

_____

_____

_____

_____

_____

_____

_____

_____

_____

_____

_____

_____

_____

_____

_____

_____

_____

_____

_____

_____

_____

_____

_____

_____

_____

_____

_____

What people say they remember about me as a child:

_____

_____

_____

_____

_____

_____

_____

_____

_____

_____

_____

_____

_____

_____

_____

_____

_____

_____

_____

_____

_____

_____

_____

_____

_____

_____

_____

_____

_____

_____

_____

My birth or nurturing mother's name and birth
date is (was). I felt and thought she:

_____

_____

_____

_____

_____

_____

_____

_____

_____

_____

_____

_____

_____

_____

_____

_____

_____

_____

_____

_____

_____

_____

_____

_____

_____

_____

_____

_____

_____

_____

_____

The person in my family who appeared to be in control most
of the time was. They took control by. I thought they were:

_____

_____

_____

_____

_____

_____

_____

_____

_____

_____

_____

_____

_____

_____

_____

_____

_____

_____

_____

_____

_____

_____

_____

_____

_____

_____

_____

_____

_____

_____

_____

_____

The person(s) who cooked the meals in
my family, my favorite dish was:

_____

_____

_____

_____

_____

_____

_____

The person(s) who taught me to cook was:

_____

_____

_____

_____

_____

_____

_____

_____

My favorite meal(s) is was:

The food(s) I really did not like:

_____

_____

_____

_____

_____

_____

_____

_____

_____

_____

_____

_____

_____

I was or was not forced to eat the food(s) I disliked:

_____

_____

_____

_____

_____

_____

_____

_____

_____

_____

_____

_____

We did or did not eat as a family because:

_____

_____

_____

_____

_____

_____

_____

_____

_____

_____

_____

_____

_____

_____

_____

_____

_____

_____

_____

_____

_____

The person(s) who taught me to comb my hair,
wash my teeth, take a bath, clean my room and
tie my shoes and how they taught me:

_____

_____

_____

_____

_____

_____

_____

_____

_____

_____

The person(s) who taught me to ride a bike,
and this is how they taught me:

_____

_____

_____

_____

_____

_____

_____

_____

_____

_____

_____

_____

_____

_____

_____

_____

When I felt sad I went to this person(s)
they would for comfort me by:

_____

_____

_____

_____

_____

_____

_____

_____

_____

_____

_____

_____

_____

_____

_____

_____

_____

_____

_____

_____

_____

_____

_____

_____

_____

_____

_____

_____

_____

This is the person(s) I felt I could always count on when I needed them; this is what and how I felt comfortable and supported by:

_____

_____

_____

_____

_____

_____

_____

_____

_____

_____

_____

_____

_____

_____

_____

_____

_____

_____

_____

_____

_____

_____

_____

_____

_____

_____

_____

_____

I was afraid of this person in my family because they:

_____

_____

_____

_____

_____

_____

_____

_____

_____

_____

_____

_____

_____

_____

_____

_____

_____

_____

_____

_____

_____

_____

_____

_____

_____

_____

_____

_____

This person betrayed me by. I felt betrayed when they did this:

_____

_____

_____

_____

_____

_____

_____

_____

_____

_____

_____

_____

_____

_____

_____

_____

_____

_____

_____

_____

_____

_____

_____

_____

_____

_____

_____

_____

This is this person(s) no matter what I did I
could not please them or understand them.
The reason(s) I believe this is because:

_____

_____

_____

_____

_____

_____

_____

_____

_____

_____

_____

_____

_____

_____

_____

_____

_____

_____

_____

_____

_____

_____

_____

_____

_____

_____

_____

_____

_____

This is the person who I felt I could never trust, because:

_____

_____

_____

_____

_____

_____

_____

_____

_____

_____

My mother's defining characteristics
(what made her different) are:

_____

_____

_____

_____

_____

_____

_____

_____

_____

_____

_____

_____

_____

_____

_____

_____

_____

_____

I was so angry when my mother or my mother figure:

_____

_____

_____

_____

_____

_____

_____

_____

_____

_____

_____

_____

_____

_____

_____

_____

_____

_____

_____

_____

_____

_____

_____

_____

_____

_____

_____

_____

_____

_____

I was so happy when my mother:

_____

_____

_____

_____

_____

_____

_____

_____

_____

_____

_____

_____

_____

_____

_____

_____

_____

_____

_____

_____

_____

_____

_____

_____

_____

_____

_____

_____

_____

What I wish my mother would have done with me:

_____

_____

_____

_____

_____

_____

_____

_____

_____

_____

_____

_____

_____

_____

_____

_____

_____

_____

I did not understand when my mother:

_____

_____

_____

_____

_____

_____

_____

_____

_____

_____

_____

_____

_____

My father's defining characteristics (what
makes him different) are:

_____

_____

_____

_____

_____

_____

_____

_____

_____

_____

_____

_____

_____

_____

_____

_____

_____

_____

_____

_____

_____

_____

_____

_____

_____

_____

_____

_____

_____

_____

I was so angry when my father:

_____

_____

_____

_____

_____

_____

_____

_____

_____

_____

_____

_____

_____

_____

_____

_____

_____

_____

_____

_____

_____

I was so happy when my father:

_____

_____

What I wish my father would have done with me:

_____

I do not understand when my father:

_____
_____
_____
_____
_____
_____
_____
_____
_____
_____
_____
_____

I felt disgusted when:

_____
_____
_____
_____
_____
_____
_____
_____
_____
_____

My relationship with my siblings (brothers and sisters) was:

_____

_____

_____

_____

_____

_____

_____

_____

_____

_____

_____

_____

_____

_____

_____

_____

_____

_____

_____

_____

_____

_____

_____

_____

_____

_____

_____

_____

_____

_____

_____

_____

My childhood pet(s) were:

_____
_____
_____
_____
_____
_____

I harmed a pet because:

_____
_____
_____
_____
_____
_____
_____

My relationship with my pet(s) was/ were:

_____
_____
_____
_____
_____
_____
_____

I never had a pet because:

_____
_____
_____
_____
_____
_____

I think pets are:

_____

_____

_____

_____

_____

_____

I like these animals because:

_____

_____

_____

_____

_____

_____

_____

I dislike these animals because:

_____

_____

_____

_____

_____

_____

_____

There were this many children in my family:

_____

_____

_____

_____

_____

_____

_____

I was the _____ (first, last, etc.,) born in my
family. I felt being born the _____ was:

_____

_____

_____

_____

_____

_____

_____

_____

_____

_____

_____

_____

_____

_____

I got along best with this sibling(s) and why:

_____

_____

_____

_____

_____

_____

I did not get along with this sibling(s) because:

_____

_____

_____

_____

_____

I admired this sibling(s) because:

_____
_____
_____
_____
_____
_____
_____
_____
_____
_____
_____
_____
_____
_____
_____

I did not like this about my sibling(s):

_____
_____
_____
_____
_____
_____
_____
_____
_____
_____
_____
_____
_____
_____
_____
_____

The situation that made me saddest is:

_____
_____
_____
_____
_____
_____
_____
_____
_____
_____
_____
_____
_____
_____
_____
_____

The situation(s) that made me scared as a young child was:

_____
_____
_____
_____
_____
_____
_____
_____
_____
_____
_____
_____
_____
_____

_____

_____

Whom I take after, or look like, and in what ways:

_____

_____

_____

_____

_____

_____

_____

_____

_____

_____

My parent(s) relationship together was:

_____

_____

_____

_____

_____

_____

_____

_____

_____

When my parents talked to each other they would:

_____

_____

_____

_____

_____

_____

_____

When my parents talked to me they would:

_____
_____
_____
_____
_____
_____
_____
_____
_____
_____
_____
_____
_____

When my parents talked to my sibling(s) they would:

_____
_____
_____
_____
_____
_____
_____
_____
_____
_____
_____
_____
_____

I was confused when my parents:

_____
_____
_____
_____
_____
_____
_____
_____
_____
_____
_____
_____
_____

I wished my parents had:

_____
_____
_____
_____
_____
_____
_____
_____
_____
_____
_____
_____
_____
_____

Disappointment is defined as an expectation that was not fulfilled. For example, "my mother was never there for me the way I wanted." "I hoped to have a happy life but I am miserable." "I thought my parents were supposed to take care of me, they did not, so why did they have me." "I wanted to get on the team and they did not pick me, what is wrong with me?"

I was so disappointed when my parents:

_____

_____

_____

_____

_____

_____

_____

_____

_____

_____

_____

_____

_____

_____

_____

_____

_____

_____

_____

_____

_____

_____

_____

_____

_____

My mother's mother is/was as I remember
her to be? Or as I was told she was:

_____
_____
_____
_____
_____
_____
_____
_____
_____
_____
_____
_____
_____
_____
_____
_____
_____
_____
_____
_____
_____
_____
_____
_____
_____
_____
_____
_____
_____
_____

My relationship with my mother's mother was:

_____
_____
_____
_____
_____
_____
_____
_____
_____
_____
_____
_____
_____
_____
_____
_____
_____
_____
_____
_____
_____
_____
_____
_____
_____
_____
_____
_____
_____

Grief is defined as an intense and sudden onset of sorrow resulting from a loss. A reaction from a loss is usually experienced as an intense emotional pain, beginning with confusion, shock, and denial. Grief is a normal part of being human.

When I was a child this person went away and I was so sad and lonely, I felt like this, I did not understand this:

_____
_____
_____
_____
_____
_____
_____
_____
_____
_____
_____
_____
_____
_____
_____
_____
_____
_____
_____
_____
_____
_____
_____
_____
_____
_____
_____
_____
_____
_____

When I was a child this person(s) died and this is how I felt:

_____

_____

_____

_____

_____

_____

_____

_____

_____

_____

_____

_____

_____

_____

_____

_____

_____

_____

_____

_____

_____

_____

_____

_____

_____

_____

_____

_____

_____

What was confusing about this person(s) death was:

_____

_____

_____

_____

_____

_____

_____

_____

_____

_____

_____

_____

_____

_____

_____

_____

_____

_____

_____

_____

_____

_____

_____

_____

_____

_____

_____

_____

_____

_____

_____

_____

My mother's father is /was I remember
him to be, or as I was told he was:

_____
_____
_____
_____
_____
_____
_____
_____
_____
_____
_____
_____
_____
_____
_____
_____
_____
_____
_____
_____
_____
_____
_____
_____
_____
_____
_____
_____
_____
_____

My relationship with my mother's father was:

_____
_____
_____
_____
_____
_____
_____
_____
_____
_____
_____
_____
_____
_____
_____
_____
_____
_____
_____
_____
_____
_____
_____
_____
_____
_____
_____
_____
_____
_____

My father's mother is/was I remember her
to be, or as I was told she was:

_____
_____
_____
_____
_____
_____
_____
_____
_____
_____
_____
_____
_____
_____
_____
_____
_____
_____
_____
_____
_____
_____
_____
_____
_____
_____
_____
_____
_____
_____

A relationship is defined as a state of being mutually or reciprocally interested. There is some kind of connection and or involvement between at least two people. Of course relationships can be empowering or disempowering. They can be healthy or unhealthy.

My relationship with my father's mother was:

_____
_____
_____
_____
_____
_____
_____
_____
_____
_____
_____
_____
_____
_____
_____
_____
_____
_____
_____
_____
_____
_____
_____
_____
_____
_____
_____
_____
_____
_____

My father's father is/was I remember him
to be, or as I was told he was:

_____
_____
_____
_____
_____
_____
_____
_____
_____
_____
_____
_____
_____
_____
_____
_____
_____
_____
_____
_____
_____
_____
_____
_____
_____
_____
_____
_____
_____
_____
_____
_____

My relationship with my father's father was:

_____
_____
_____
_____
_____
_____
_____
_____
_____
_____
_____
_____
_____
_____
_____
_____
_____
_____
_____
_____
_____
_____
_____
_____
_____
_____
_____
_____
_____

The meaning of our family name is:

_____

_____

_____

_____

_____

_____

_____

_____

_____

_____

_____

_____

_____

_____

This is my definition of what a family should be (my fantasy)

_____

_____

_____

_____

_____

_____

_____

_____

_____

_____

_____

_____

_____

_____

This is what my family was like:

_____
_____
_____
_____
_____
_____
_____
_____
_____
_____
_____
_____
_____
_____
_____
_____
_____
_____
_____
_____
_____
_____
_____
_____
_____
_____
_____
_____

I would say my family was healthy or unhealthy because:

_____
_____
_____
_____
_____
_____
_____
_____
_____
_____
_____
_____
_____
_____
_____
_____
_____
_____
_____
_____
_____
_____
_____
_____
_____
_____
_____
_____
_____
_____

When I went to my friend's house and experienced their family I was surprised they did:

_____

_____

_____

_____

_____

_____

_____

_____

_____

_____

_____

_____

_____

_____

_____

_____

_____

_____

_____

_____

_____

_____

_____

_____

_____

_____

_____

_____

_____

If I had a magic wand I would do this to my family:

_____

_____

_____

_____

_____

_____

_____

_____

_____

_____

_____

_____

_____

_____

_____

_____

_____

_____

_____

_____

_____

_____

_____

_____

_____

_____

_____

_____

I was embarrassed that my family:

_____
_____
_____
_____
_____
_____
_____
_____
_____
_____
_____
_____
_____
_____
_____
_____
_____
_____
_____
_____
_____
_____
_____
_____
_____
_____
_____
_____
_____
_____
_____
_____
_____

I was proud of my family when:

_____
_____
_____
_____
_____
_____
_____
_____
_____
_____
_____
_____
_____
_____
_____
_____
_____
_____
_____
_____
_____
_____
_____
_____
_____
_____
_____
_____

Where my family originally came from:

_____
_____
_____
_____
_____
_____
_____
_____
_____
_____
_____
_____
_____
_____
_____
_____
_____
_____
_____
_____
_____
_____
_____
_____
_____
_____

My family made family decisions by:

_____

_____

_____

_____

_____

_____

_____

_____

_____

_____

_____

_____

_____

_____

_____

_____

_____

_____

_____

_____

_____

_____

_____

_____

_____

_____

_____

_____

_____

_____

_____

My family resolved problems by:

_____
_____
_____
_____
_____
_____
_____
_____
_____
_____
_____
_____
_____
_____
_____
_____
_____
_____
_____
_____
_____
_____
_____
_____
_____
_____
_____
_____
_____

The most racist thing I heard a family member say
about another race was and I felt the comment was:

_____
_____
_____
_____
_____
_____
_____
_____
_____
_____
_____
_____
_____
_____
_____
_____
_____
_____
_____
_____
_____
_____
_____
_____
_____
_____
_____
_____
_____
_____
_____
_____
_____

My family had family gatherings (reunions,
Christmas, thanksgiving):

_____

_____

_____

_____

_____

_____

_____

_____

_____

_____

_____

_____

_____

_____

_____

_____

_____

_____

_____

_____

_____

_____

_____

_____

_____

_____

_____

_____

_____

_____

This person in my family pointed out everyone's problems:

_____
_____
_____
_____
_____
_____
_____
_____
_____
_____
_____
_____
_____
_____
_____
_____
_____
_____
_____
_____
_____
_____
_____
_____
_____
_____
_____
_____
_____
_____
_____
_____

Race is defined as a family, tribe, people, or nation belonging to the same stock. A race is a class or kind of people unified; by their communities, their areas of interest, their habits, and/ or their characteristics. Culture is defined as the integrated pattern of human behavior that includes thought, speech, action, and artifacts and depends upon man's (human's) capacity for learning and transmitting knowledge to succeeding generations. A culture holds customary beliefs, social forms, and material traits of a racial, religious, or social group.

My race and cultural origins are:

_____
_____
_____
_____
_____
_____
_____
_____
_____
_____
_____
_____
_____
_____
_____
_____
_____
_____
_____
_____
_____
_____
_____

The language(s) spoken in my home was/ is:

_____
_____
_____
_____
_____
_____
_____
_____
_____
_____
_____
_____
_____
_____
_____
_____
_____
_____
_____
_____
_____
_____
_____
_____
_____
_____
_____
_____
_____
_____

Who's who?
My family consisted of these people: Families are diverse so please include all the people who you call your family.

<u>Name(s):</u>   <u>Relationship to You:</u>

_____

_____

_____

_____

_____

_____

_____

_____

_____

_____

_____

_____

_____

_____

_____

_____

_____

_____

You may also diagram your family of origin by drawing a genogram.

Genograms were first developed and popularized in clinical settings by Monica McGoldrick and Randy Gerson through the publication of a book titled *Genograms: Assessment and Intervention* in 1985. Genograms are used illuminate family dynamics (Jolly, Froom Rosen, 1980). YouTube tutorial below, however is as *simple as hand drawing on a piece of paper.*

- <u>Genogram & Eco Map Tutorial - Microsoft Word - YouTube</u>

Where I lived as a child:

_____
_____
_____
_____
_____
_____
_____
_____
_____
_____
_____
_____
_____
_____
_____
_____
_____
_____
_____
_____
_____
_____
_____
_____
_____
_____
_____
_____
_____

A neighborhood is a place or region in close proximity, where there are people living near one another. A neighborhood can have a culture; the culture could be friendly and supportive, or it could be distant and/or hostile and violent.

The neighborhood was:

_____

_____

_____

_____

_____

_____

_____

_____

_____

_____

_____

_____

_____

_____

_____

_____

_____

_____

_____

_____

_____

_____

_____

_____

_____

My best memories of the neighborhood were:

_____
_____
_____
_____
_____
_____
_____
_____
_____
_____
_____
_____
_____
_____
_____
_____
_____
_____
_____
_____
_____
_____
_____
_____
_____
_____
_____
_____

My worst memories of the neighborhood were:

_____
_____
_____
_____
_____
_____
_____
_____
_____
_____
_____
_____
_____
_____
_____
_____
_____
_____
_____
_____
_____
_____
_____
_____
_____
_____
_____
_____
_____
_____
_____
_____

A family is defined as a group of people of common ancestry. The family is considered the basic unit in society. Families have become very diverse.

The faith (religious denomination) in
which my family practiced:

_____

_____

_____

_____

_____

_____

_____

_____

_____

_____

_____

_____

_____

_____

_____

_____

_____

_____

_____

_____

_____

_____

_____

_____

_____

_____

_____

_____

_____

_____

How I felt about the faith my family practiced:

_____

_____

_____

_____

_____

_____

_____

_____

_____

_____

_____

_____

_____

_____

_____

_____

_____

_____

_____

_____

_____

_____

_____

_____

_____

_____

_____

The faith (religion) I practice today:

_____
_____
_____
_____
_____
_____
_____
_____
_____
_____
_____
_____
_____
_____
_____
_____
_____
_____
_____
_____
_____
_____
_____
_____
_____
_____
_____
_____
_____
_____
_____
_____

Special family or religious holidays we celebrated
when I was a child that I still cherish:

_____

_____

_____

_____

_____

_____

_____

_____

_____

_____

_____

_____

_____

_____

_____

_____

_____

_____

_____

_____

_____

_____

_____

_____

_____

_____

_____

_____

_____

_____

My favorite holiday(s) was:

_____
_____
_____
_____
_____
_____
_____
_____
_____
_____
_____
_____
_____
_____
_____
_____
_____
_____
_____
_____
_____
_____
_____
_____
_____
_____
_____

On this holiday(s) my family would:

_____
_____
_____
_____
_____
_____
_____
_____
_____
_____
_____
_____
_____
_____
_____
_____
_____
_____
_____
_____
_____
_____
_____
_____
_____
_____
_____
_____
_____
_____

My families favorite weekend thing(s) to do was:

_____
_____
_____
_____
_____
_____
_____
_____
_____
_____
_____
_____
_____
_____
_____
_____
_____
_____
_____
_____
_____
_____
_____
_____
_____
_____
_____
_____
_____

My aunts and uncles:

_____
_____
_____
_____
_____
_____
_____
_____
_____
_____
_____
_____
_____
_____
_____
_____
_____
_____
_____
_____
_____
_____
_____
_____
_____
_____
_____
_____
_____
_____
_____

My extended family (cousins, nieces, nephews):

_____
_____
_____
_____
_____
_____
_____
_____
_____
_____
_____
_____
_____
_____
_____
_____
_____
_____
_____
_____
_____
_____
_____
_____
_____
_____
_____
_____
_____
_____

The relationship(s) I had with my extended family was:

_____

_____

_____

_____

_____

_____

_____

_____

_____

_____

_____

_____

_____

_____

_____

_____

_____

_____

_____

_____

_____

_____

_____

_____

_____

_____

_____

_____

_____

_____

_____

What made my extended family special or not:

_____
_____
_____
_____
_____
_____
_____
_____
_____
_____
_____
_____
_____
_____
_____
_____
_____
_____
_____
_____
_____
_____
_____
_____
_____
_____

The person(s) in my family that was most
talked about (good or bad):

_____
_____
_____
_____
_____
_____
_____
_____
_____
_____
_____
_____
_____
_____
_____
_____
_____
_____
_____
_____
_____
_____
_____
_____
_____
_____
_____
_____
_____
_____

The person(s) in my family that I looked up to as a role model(s):

_____

_____

_____

_____

_____

_____

_____

_____

_____

_____

_____

_____

_____

_____

_____

_____

_____

_____

_____

_____

_____

_____

_____

_____

_____

_____

_____

_____

_____

They taught me to:

_____
_____
_____
_____
_____
_____
_____
_____
_____
_____
_____
_____
_____
_____
_____
_____
_____
_____
_____
_____
_____
_____
_____
_____
_____
_____
_____
_____
_____
_____
_____

I appreciate how they:

_____
_____
_____
_____
_____
_____
_____
_____
_____
_____
_____
_____
_____
_____
_____
_____
_____
_____
_____
_____
_____
_____
_____
_____
_____
_____
_____
_____
_____
_____

This is what I learned about employment from my family:

_____
_____
_____
_____
_____
_____
_____
_____
_____
_____
_____
_____
_____
_____
_____
_____
_____
_____
_____
_____
_____
_____
_____
_____
_____
_____
_____
_____
_____
_____

This what I learned about drug and alcohol from my family:

_____
_____
_____
_____
_____
_____
_____
_____
_____
_____
_____
_____
_____
_____
_____
_____
_____
_____
_____
_____
_____
_____
_____
_____
_____
_____
_____
_____
_____

This is what I learned about food from my family:

_____

_____

_____

_____

_____

_____

_____

_____

_____

_____

_____

_____

_____

_____

_____

_____

_____

_____

_____

_____

_____

_____

_____

_____

_____

_____

_____

_____

_____

_____

This is what I learned about religion from my family:

_____
_____
_____
_____
_____
_____
_____
_____
_____
_____
_____
_____
_____
_____
_____
_____
_____
_____
_____
_____
_____
_____
_____
_____
_____
_____
_____
_____

This is what I learned about hope from my family:

_____
_____
_____
_____
_____
_____
_____
_____
_____
_____
_____
_____
_____
_____
_____
_____
_____
_____
_____
_____
_____
_____
_____
_____
_____
_____
_____
_____
_____
_____
_____
_____
_____
_____

This is what I learned about dreams from my family:

_____
_____
_____
_____
_____
_____
_____
_____
_____
_____
_____
_____
_____
_____
_____
_____
_____
_____
_____
_____
_____
_____
_____
_____
_____
_____
_____
_____
_____
_____
_____
_____
_____

This is what I learned about love from my family:

_____
_____
_____
_____
_____
_____
_____
_____
_____
_____
_____
_____
_____
_____
_____
_____
_____
_____
_____
_____
_____
_____
_____
_____
_____
_____
_____
_____
_____
_____
_____
_____

This is what I learned about morals from my family:

_____

_____

_____

_____

_____

_____

_____

_____

_____

_____

_____

_____

_____

_____

_____

_____

_____

_____

_____

_____

_____

_____

_____

_____

_____

_____

_____

_____

This is what I learned about independence from my family

_____

_____

_____

_____

_____

_____

_____

_____

_____

_____

_____

_____

_____

_____

_____

_____

_____

_____

_____

_____

_____

_____

_____

_____

_____

_____

_____

_____

_____

_____

_____

_____

_____

This is what I learned about resolving conflicts from my family

_____

_____

_____

_____

_____

_____

_____

_____

_____

_____

_____

_____

_____

_____

_____

_____

_____

_____

_____

_____

_____

_____

_____

_____

_____

_____

_____

_____

_____

This is what I learned about sex from my family:

_____
_____
_____
_____
_____
_____
_____
_____
_____
_____
_____
_____
_____
_____
_____
_____
_____
_____
_____
_____
_____
_____
_____
_____
_____
_____
_____
_____
_____
_____

This is what I learned about intimate
relationships from my family:

_____

_____

_____

_____

_____

_____

_____

_____

_____

_____

_____

_____

_____

_____

_____

_____

_____

_____

_____

_____

_____

_____

_____

_____

_____

_____

This is what I learned about life from my family:

_____
_____
_____
_____
_____
_____
_____
_____
_____
_____
_____
_____
_____
_____
_____
_____
_____
_____
_____
_____
_____
_____
_____
_____
_____
_____
_____
_____
_____
_____
_____
_____

This is what I learned about the opposite sex from my family:

_____
_____
_____
_____
_____
_____
_____
_____
_____
_____
_____
_____
_____
_____
_____
_____
_____
_____
_____
_____
_____
_____
_____
_____
_____
_____
_____
_____
_____
_____
_____

This is what I learned about health from my family:

_____
_____
_____
_____
_____
_____
_____
_____
_____
_____
_____
_____
_____
_____
_____
_____
_____
_____
_____
_____
_____
_____
_____
_____
_____
_____
_____
_____
_____

This is what I learned about success from my family:

_____
_____
_____
_____
_____
_____
_____
_____
_____
_____
_____
_____
_____
_____
_____
_____
_____
_____
_____
_____
_____
_____
_____
_____
_____
_____
_____
_____
_____
_____
_____

This is what I learned about domestic violence from my family:

_____
_____
_____
_____
_____
_____
_____
_____
_____
_____
_____
_____
_____
_____
_____
_____
_____
_____
_____
_____
_____
_____
_____
_____
_____
_____
_____
_____
_____
_____
_____
_____

This is what I learned about other races
and cultures from my family:

_____

_____

_____

_____

_____

_____

_____

_____

_____

_____

_____

_____

_____

_____

_____

_____

_____

_____

_____

_____

_____

_____

_____

_____

_____

_____

_____

_____

_____

_____

_____

_____

_____

This is what I learned about commitment from my family:

_____

_____

_____

_____

_____

_____

_____

_____

_____

_____

_____

_____

_____

_____

_____

_____

_____

_____

_____

_____

_____

_____

_____

_____

_____

_____

_____

_____

_____

_____

_____

_____

This is what I learned about responsibility from my family:

This is what I learned about education from my family:

_____

_____

_____

_____

_____

_____

_____

_____

_____

_____

_____

_____

_____

_____

_____

_____

_____

_____

_____

_____

_____

_____

_____

_____

_____

_____

_____

_____

_____

_____

This is what I learned about worry from my family:

_____
_____
_____
_____
_____
_____
_____
_____
_____
_____
_____
_____
_____
_____
_____
_____
_____
_____
_____
_____
_____
_____
_____
_____
_____
_____
_____
_____
_____
_____

This is what I learned about puberty from my family:

_____
_____
_____
_____
_____
_____
_____
_____
_____
_____
_____
_____
_____
_____
_____
_____
_____
_____
_____
_____
_____
_____
_____
_____
_____
_____
_____
_____
_____
_____
_____

This is what I learned about marriage from my family:

_____

_____

_____

_____

_____

_____

_____

_____

_____

_____

_____

_____

_____

_____

_____

_____

_____

_____

_____

_____

_____

_____

_____

_____

_____

_____

_____

_____

_____

_____

_____

_____

This is what I learned about divorce from my family:

_____

_____

_____

_____

_____

_____

_____

_____

_____

_____

_____

_____

_____

_____

_____

_____

_____

_____

_____

_____

_____

_____

_____

_____

_____

_____

_____

_____

_____

This is what I learned about death from my family:

_____
_____
_____
_____
_____
_____
_____
_____
_____
_____
_____
_____
_____
_____
_____
_____
_____
_____
_____
_____
_____
_____
_____
_____
_____
_____
_____
_____
_____
_____
_____
_____
_____
_____

This is what I learned about compassion from my family:

_____
_____
_____
_____
_____
_____
_____
_____
_____
_____
_____
_____
_____
_____
_____
_____
_____
_____
_____
_____
_____
_____
_____
_____
_____
_____
_____
_____
_____
_____
_____
_____
_____

This is what I learned about fighting (arguing, disagreements, solving conflicts) from my family:

_____

_____

_____

_____

_____

_____

_____

_____

_____

_____

_____

_____

_____

_____

_____

_____

_____

_____

_____

_____

_____

_____

_____

_____

_____

_____

_____

_____

_____

This is what I learned about delayed
gratification from my family:

_____
_____
_____
_____
_____
_____
_____
_____
_____
_____
_____
_____
_____
_____
_____
_____
_____
_____
_____
_____
_____
_____
_____
_____
_____
_____
_____
_____
_____
_____
_____
_____

This is what I learned about sexually
transmitted diseases from my family

_____

_____
_____
_____
_____
_____
_____
_____
_____
_____
_____
_____
_____
_____
_____
_____
_____
_____
_____
_____
_____
_____
_____
_____
_____
_____
_____
_____
_____
_____
_____
_____
_____

This is what I learned about life struggles from my family

This is what I learned about grief from my family

_____

_____

_____

_____

_____

_____

_____

_____

_____

_____

_____

_____

_____

_____

_____

_____

_____

_____

_____

_____

_____

_____

_____

_____

_____

_____

_____

Hurtfulness is defined as the infliction of physical, mental, emotional, spiritual pain on another human being. Neglect is defined as the act of giving little attention or respect to another human being, as well as leaving something undone or unattended to especially by careless indifference. Abandonment is defined as a complete disinterest in the fate of another person where there has been a relationship.

The person(s) in my family that really hurt me

_____

_____

_____

_____

_____

_____

_____

_____

_____

_____

_____

_____

_____

_____

_____

_____

_____

_____

_____

_____

_____

_____

_____

_____

_____

_____

_____

A Social Worker and/or a Police Officer
came to my house because

_____

_____
_____
_____
_____
_____
_____
_____
_____
_____
_____
_____
_____
_____
_____
_____
_____
_____
_____
_____
_____
_____
_____
_____
_____

I was really hurt by the person(s) when they did this to me:

_____
_____
_____
_____
_____
_____
_____
_____

_____

_____

_____

_____

_____

_____

_____

_____

_____

_____

I have been told I have to forgive the person(s)
but this is what I cannot forget:

_____

_____

_____

_____

_____

_____

_____

_____

_____

_____

_____

As a child I thought this about the person(s) who hurt me:

_____

_____

_____

_____

_____

_____

_____

_____

_____

_____

_____

_____

_____

_____

_____

_____

_____

I thought this about me when I was hurt by this person(s):

_____

_____

_____

_____

_____

_____

_____

_____

_____

_____

_____

This is what I thought about the hurtful
things that happen to me:

_____

_____

_____

_____

_____

_____

_____

_____

_____

_____

_____

_____

_____

_____

_____

_____

_____

_____

This is what I thought I had done to deserve the hurt:

_____

_____

_____

_____

_____

_____

_____

_____

_____

_____

_____

This what I felt about the person(s) who hurt me:

_____

_____

_____

_____

_____

_____

_____

_____

_____

_____

_____

_____

_____

_____

_____

_____

_____

_____

This is what I wanted to tell the person(s) who hurt me:

_____

_____

_____

_____

_____

_____

_____

_____

_____

_____

_____

This is what I wanted to do to the person(s) who hurt me:

_____

_____

_____

_____

_____

_____

_____

_____

_____

_____

_____

_____

_____

_____

_____

_____

_____

_____

This is who I wanted to tell about my hurt:

_____

_____

_____

_____

_____

_____

_____

_____

_____

This is why I think I did not tell someone
what the person(s) did to me:

_____

_____

_____

_____

_____

_____

_____

_____

_____

_____

_____

_____

_____

This is who I told about the person(s) who hurt me:

_____

_____

_____

_____

_____

This is what they did or did not do to the
person(s) who hurt me when I told them:

_____

_____

_____

_____

_____

_____

_____

_____

_____

After I told them I felt:

_____

_____

_____

_____

_____

_____

_____

_____

_____

_____

_____

_____

_____

_____

_____

After I told them this is what I thought:

_____

_____

_____

_____

_____

_____

_____

_____

_____

_____

_____

_____

_____

_____

_____

_____

After I told them I felt I did the right thing because:

_____

_____

_____

_____

_____

_____

I felt I did the wrong thing because:

After I told them I felt I got justice by:

_____
_____
_____
_____
_____
_____
_____
_____
_____
_____
_____
_____
_____
_____
_____
_____
_____
_____
_____
_____
_____
_____
_____
_____
_____
_____
_____

After I told them I regretted it because:

_____

_____

_____

_____

_____

_____

_____

_____

_____

_____

_____

_____

_____

Define all types of violence you have experienced

The worst violent incident that I can
remember when I was young:

_____

_____

_____

_____

_____

_____

_____

_____

_____

_____

_____

_____

_____

This is the physical violence I witnessed between
my parents when I was growing up:

_____
_____
_____
_____
_____
_____
_____
_____
_____
_____
_____
_____
_____
_____

When I witnessed physical violence between my parents I felt:

_____
_____
_____
_____
_____
_____
_____
_____
_____
_____
_____
_____
_____
_____
_____

When I witnessed physical violence
between my parents I thought:

_____

_____

_____

_____

_____

_____

_____

_____

_____

_____

_____

_____

When I witnessed physical violence between
my parents this is what I did:

_____

_____

_____

_____

_____

_____

_____

_____

_____

_____

_____

_____

When I witnessed physical violence between my parents this is how I **felt** about my father:

_____
_____
_____
_____
_____
_____
_____
_____
_____
_____
_____
_____
_____
_____
_____
_____
_____
_____
_____
_____
_____
_____
_____
_____
_____
_____
_____
_____
_____
_____

When I witnessed physical violence between my
parents this is what I wanted to do to my father:

_____
_____
_____
_____
_____
_____
_____
_____
_____
_____
_____
_____
_____
_____

This is what I **thought** about my father:

_____
_____
_____
_____
_____
_____
_____
_____
_____
_____
_____
_____
_____
_____

When I witnessed physical violence between my
parents this is how I **felt** about my mother:

_____
_____
_____
_____
_____
_____
_____
_____
_____
_____
_____
_____
_____
_____
_____
_____

When I witnessed physical violence between my
parents this is what I wanted to do to my mother:

_____
_____
_____
_____
_____
_____
_____
_____
_____
_____
_____
_____

This is what I **thought** about my mother:

_____

_____

_____

_____

_____

_____

_____

_____

_____

_____

_____

_____

_____

_____

This was the emotional and mental violence, I witnessed
between my parents, when I was growing up:

_____

_____

_____

_____

_____

_____

_____

_____

_____

_____

_____

_____

_____

_____

When I witnessed emotional, mental
violence between my parents I felt:

_____

_____

_____

_____

_____

_____

_____

_____

_____

_____

_____

_____

_____

_____

When I witnessed emotional, mental violence
between my parents I thought:

_____

_____

_____

_____

_____

_____

_____

_____

_____

_____

_____

_____

_____

_____

_____

When I witnessed emotional, mental violence
between my parents this is what I did:

_____

_____

_____

_____

_____

_____

_____

_____

_____

_____

_____

_____

_____

When I witnessed emotional, mental violence between
my parents this is how I **felt** about my father:

_____

_____

_____

_____

_____

_____

_____

_____

_____

_____

_____

_____

_____

_____

When I witnessed emotional mental violence between my parents this is what I wanted to do to my father:

_____
_____
_____
_____
_____
_____
_____
_____
_____
_____
_____
_____
_____
_____
_____

This is what I **thought** about my father:

_____
_____
_____
_____
_____
_____
_____
_____
_____
_____
_____
_____
_____
_____
_____
_____
_____

When I witnessed emotional, mental violence between
my parents this is how I **felt** about my mother:

_____
_____
_____
_____
_____
_____
_____
_____
_____
_____
_____
_____
_____
_____
_____

When I witnessed emotional, mental violence between
my parents this is what I wanted to do to my mother:

_____
_____
_____
_____
_____
_____
_____
_____
_____
_____
_____
_____

This is what I **thought** about my mother:

_____
_____
_____
_____
_____
_____
_____
_____
_____
_____
_____
_____
_____
_____
_____
_____
_____
_____

In my opinion my parents were physically, mentally, and emotionally abuse to me by these actions:

_____
_____
_____
_____
_____
_____
_____
_____
_____
_____
_____
_____
_____

_____
_____
_____
_____
_____
_____
_____
_____
_____
_____
_____
_____

The person(s) that told me the best stories
was, my favorite story(s) was/were:

_____
_____
_____
_____
_____
_____
_____
_____
_____
_____
_____
_____
_____
_____
_____
_____
_____
_____
_____
_____
_____

The person(s) who could make me laugh was, and this is why:

_____
_____
_____
_____
_____
_____
_____
_____
_____
_____
_____
_____
_____
_____
_____
_____

The person(s) who I felt loved me unconditionally was:

_____
_____
_____
_____
_____
_____
_____
_____
_____
_____
_____
_____

_____

_____

_____

_____

_____

_____

_____

_____

_____

_____

_____

The person(s) I could trust was and why:

_____

_____

_____

_____

_____

_____

_____

_____

_____

_____

_____

_____

_____

_____

_____

_____

_____

_____

_____

_____

_____

_____

_____

_____

_____

_____

_____

_____

_____

_____

_____

_____

The best advice that I was given as a child was:

_____

_____

_____

_____

_____

_____

_____

_____

_____

_____

_____

_____

_____

_____

_____

_____

_____

_____

_____

_____

_____

_____

_____

_____

_____

_____

_____

_____

_____

The person(s) that gave me the advice was, I believe he/she:

_____

_____

_____

_____

_____

_____

_____

_____

_____

_____

_____

_____

_____

_____

_____

_____

_____

The worst (hardest experience) lesson that
I really learned a lot from was:

_____

_____

_____

_____

_____

_____

_____

_____

_____

_____

_____

_____

_____

_____

_____

_____

_____

_____

_____

*If I can understand my life history objectively (the facts) I can
begin to help myself come to understand my subjectivity (my
feelings) and then I can begin to live, the who I am today!*

**Looking back at my life history objectively
I have a clearer understanding of:**

_____

_____

_____

_____

_____

_____

_____

_____

_____

_____

_____

_____

_____

_____

_____

_____

_____

_____

_____

_____

_____

_____

_____

_____

_____

_____

_____

_____

**Looking back at my life history objectively
I have a clearer understanding of:**

_____

_____

_____

_____

_____

_____

_____

_____

_____

_____

_____

_____

_____

_____

_____

_____

_____

_____

_____

_____

_____

_____

_____

_____

_____

_____

_____

_____

**Looking back at my life history objectively
I have a clearer understanding of:**

_____

_____

_____

_____

_____

_____

_____

_____

_____

_____

_____

_____

_____

_____

_____

_____

_____

_____

_____

_____

_____

_____

_____

_____

_____

_____

_____

_____

_____

**Looking back at my life history objectively
I have a clearer understanding of:**

_____

_____

_____

_____

_____

_____

_____

_____

_____

_____

_____

_____

_____

_____

_____

_____

_____

_____

_____

_____

_____

_____

_____

_____

_____

_____

**Looking back at my life history objectively
I have a clearer understanding of:**

_____

_____

_____

_____

_____

_____

_____

_____

_____

_____

_____

_____

_____

_____

_____

_____

_____

_____

_____

_____

_____

_____

_____

_____

_____

_____

_____

_____

_____

**Looking back at my life history objectively
I have a clearer understanding of:**

_____

_____

_____

_____

_____

_____

_____

_____

_____

_____

_____

_____

_____

_____

_____

_____

_____

_____

_____

_____

_____

_____

_____

_____

_____

_____

_____

_____

_____

**Looking back at my life history objectively
I have a clearer understanding of:**

_____

_____

_____

_____

_____

_____

_____

_____

_____

_____

_____

_____

_____

_____

_____

_____

_____

_____

_____

_____

_____

_____

_____

_____

_____

_____

_____

Looking back at my life history objectively
I have a clearer understanding of:

_____

_____

_____

_____

_____

_____

_____

_____

_____

_____

_____

_____

_____

_____

_____

_____

_____

_____

_____

_____

_____

_____

_____

_____

_____

_____

_____

_____

_____

_____

**Looking back at my life history objectively
I have a clearer understanding of:**

_____

_____

_____

_____

_____

_____

_____

_____

_____

_____

_____

_____

_____

_____

_____

_____

_____

_____

_____

_____

_____

_____

_____

_____

_____

_____

_____

_____

_____

_____

**Looking back at my life history objectively
I have a clearer understanding of:**

_____

_____

_____

_____

_____

_____

_____

_____

_____

_____

_____

_____

_____

_____

_____

_____

_____

_____

_____

_____

_____

_____

_____

_____

_____

_____

_____

_____

_____

_____

**Looking back at my life history objectively
I have a clearer understanding of:**

_____

_____

_____

_____

_____

_____

_____

_____

_____

_____

_____

_____

_____

_____

_____

_____

_____

_____

_____

_____

_____

_____

_____

_____

_____

_____

_____

_____

_____

_____

**Looking back at my life history objectively
I have a clearer understanding of:**

_____

_____

_____

_____

_____

_____

_____

_____

_____

_____

_____

_____

_____

_____

_____

_____

_____

_____

_____

_____

_____

_____

_____

_____

_____

_____

_____

_____

_____

_____

**Looking back at my life history objectively
I have a clearer understanding of:**

_____

_____

_____

_____

_____

_____

_____

_____

_____

_____

_____

_____

_____

_____

_____

_____

_____

_____

_____

_____

_____

_____

_____

_____

_____

_____

_____

**Looking back at my life history objectively
I have a clearer understanding of:**

_____

_____

_____

_____

_____

_____

_____

_____

_____

_____

_____

_____

_____

_____

_____

_____

_____

_____

_____

_____

_____

_____

_____

_____

_____

_____

_____

_____

_____

**Looking back at my life history objectively
I have a clearer understanding of:**

_____

_____

_____

_____

_____

_____

_____

_____

_____

_____

_____

_____

_____

_____

_____

_____

_____

_____

_____

_____

_____

_____

_____

_____

_____

_____

_____

_____

_____

**Looking back at my life history objectively
I have a clearer understanding of:**

_____

_____

_____

_____

_____

_____

_____

_____

_____

_____

_____

_____

_____

_____

_____

_____

_____

_____
_____
_____
_____
_____
_____
_____
_____
_____
_____
_____
_____
_____

So many times I have heard that it is best to forgive and forget! Yet, the words seemed so cheap, and foreign to my pain, easy to say but the process is hard to do. The truth is resolution is the key to freedom which leads me back to me.

Looking back at my life history I can forgive because I now understand:

_____
_____
_____
_____
_____
_____
_____
_____
_____
_____
_____
_____

_____

_____

_____

_____

_____

_____

_____

_____

_____

_____

_____

_____

_____

_____

Looking back at my life history I can forgive because I now understand:

_____

_____

_____

_____

_____

_____

_____

_____

_____

_____

_____

_____

_____

_____

_____

_____

_____

_____

_____

_____

_____

_____

_____

_____

_____

_____

_____

_____

_____

_____

_____

**Looking back at my life history I can
forgive because I now understand:**

_____

_____

_____

_____

_____

_____

_____

_____

_____

_____

_____

_____

_____

_____

_____

_____

_____

_____

_____

_____

_____

_____

_____

_____

_____

_____

_____

_____

_____

_____

**Looking back at my life history I can
forgive because I now understand:**

_____

_____

_____

_____

_____

_____

_____

_____

_____

_____

_____

_____

_____

_____

_____

_____

_____

_____

_____

_____

_____

_____

_____

_____

_____

_____

_____

_____

_____

_____

**Looking back at my life history I can
forgive because I now understand:**

_____

_____

_____

_____

_____

_____

_____

_____

_____

_____

_____

_____

_____

_____

_____

_____

_____

_____

_____

_____

_____

_____

_____

_____

_____

_____

_____

_____

_____

_____

**Looking back at my life history I can
forgive because I now understand:**

_____

_____

_____

_____

_____

_____

_____

_____

_____

_____

_____

_____

_____

_____

_____

_____

_____

_____

_____

_____

_____

_____

_____

_____

_____

_____

_____

_____

_____

_____

**Looking back at my life history I can
forgive because I now understand:**

_____

_____

_____

_____

_____

_____

_____

_____

_____

_____

_____

_____

_____

_____

_____

_____

_____

_____

_____

_____

_____

_____

_____

_____

_____

_____

_____

_____

_____

Looking back at my life history I can forgive because I now understand:

_____

_____

_____

_____

_____

_____

_____

_____

_____

_____

_____

_____

_____

_____

_____

_____

_____

_____

_____

_____

_____

_____

_____

_____

_____

_____

_____

_____

_____

_____

**Looking back at my life history I can
forgive because I now understand:**

_____

_____

_____

_____

_____

_____

_____

_____

_____

_____

_____

_____

_____

_____

_____

_____

_____

_____

_____

_____

_____
_____
_____
_____
_____
_____
_____
_____
_____
_____
_____
_____
_____

Looking back at my life history I can forgive because I now understand:

_____
_____
_____
_____
_____
_____
_____
_____
_____
_____
_____
_____
_____
_____
_____
_____
_____
_____
_____
_____

_____
_____
_____
_____
_____
_____
_____
_____
_____
_____
_____
_____
_____

*These things I have not at this time understood. I know I
have choices I can do many things. I can either put them
on the table for another time when I decide I have the time
and energy to journey into me again. Or I can explore
them with the help of a professional. Or I can decide I
am okay with them and I can let them fly away like a
dove, with my decision to free myself once and for all.*

**Things that I still do not understand
about me and my life events:**

_____
_____
_____
_____
_____
_____
_____
_____
_____
_____
_____

_____

_____

_____

_____

_____

_____

_____

_____

_____

_____

_____

_____

Things that I still do not understand about me and my life events:

_____

_____

_____

_____

_____

_____

_____

_____

_____

_____

_____

_____

_____

_____

_____

_____

_____

_____

_____
_____
_____
_____
_____
_____
_____
_____
_____
_____
_____
_____

Take off the dis- in disappointment and you have
the word appointment left. This could be viewed as
an appointment to grow and or gain wisdom.

**Looking back at my life history I understand
how my disappointments have really been
appointments for me to gain wisdom:**

_____
_____
_____
_____
_____
_____
_____
_____
_____
_____
_____
_____

_____

_____

_____

_____

_____

_____

_____

_____

_____

_____

_____

_____

Some things we will never really understand but we can put them to rest with self-love and compassion for ourselves and others. Holding onto something for the sake of being bitter only makes us bitter.

Things that I still do not understand about me and my life events:

_____

_____

_____

_____

_____

_____

_____

_____

_____

_____

_____

_____

_____

Here I am this is me good, bad, ugly, beautiful. Here I am!

_____

_____

_____

_____

_____

_____

_____

_____

_____

_____

_____

_____

_____

_____

The End Is Only the Beginning for Me.

References

https://www.youtube.com/watch?v=ldbuM-nDcAA Nov 8, 2013. Genogram
and Eco maps.

Sobremonte, P. (2006). Therapeutic Journaling.

*W Jolly; J Froom; MG Rosen (Feb 1980), "The genogram", The genogram
(The Journal of family practice)* **10**, *pp. 251–5,* <u>PMID</u> <u>7354276</u>

Printed in the United States
By Bookmasters